MAR 23 65   (14-9104)

THE IMPACT OF AMERICA ON
EUROPEAN CULTURE

The Impact of America
on European Culture

BERTRAND RUSSELL · JOHN LEHMANN

SEAN O'FAOLAIN · J. E. MORPURGO

MARTIN COOPER · PERRY MILLER

Boston · THE BEACON PRESS · 1951

The essays in this book were originally presented, in somewhat different form, on the "Third Programme" of the British Broadcasting Corporation.

Printed in U. S. A.

Contents

1

THE POLITICAL AND CULTURAL INFLUENCE

Bertrand Russell

BERTRAND RUSSELL has obtained a first-hand knowledge of American mores during several periods of travel and residence in the United States.

BERTRAND RUSSELL

The Political and Cultural Influence

America is affecting Europe in so many ways, and
at so many different levels, that it is difficult to know
where to begin, or what kind of influence to regard as
the more important. How can we compare, and how
bring within the compass of one discourse, such dis-
parate matters as the effect of Hollywood on the minds
of shopgirls and the effect of Mr. Justice Holmes on
the mind of Mr. Laski? I cannot answer such a question. I will only say, to begin with, that Europeans
with pretensions to culture are too apt to remember
Hollywood with a sniff, and forget the respect due to
such men as Holmes, who was, after all, equally a product of America. I will try to rectify this one-sidedness
by dwelling chiefly upon the importance of America
in the world of ideas.

What America stood for in the minds of Europeans
of the early nineteenth century was, in many ways,
the exact opposite of what America stands for at the
present day. From 1776 to the death of Lincoln,
America was the Mecca of Radicals, the only large
country where democracy was successfully practiced.

3

Now America has become the bulwark of capitalism, the main hope of those who dread the advancing tide of socialism and communism, and the chief promise of stability amid the kaleidoscopic transformations that bewilder the puzzled inhabitants of Europe and Asia. I once lectured in New York in a building called the "Hall of Liberty," erected by German Radicals who fled from their native country after the failure of the Revolution of 1848. Their portraits hung on the walls, and among them was the father of Heinz of the 57 varieties. The contrast between what the father hoped of America and what the son made of it (and out of it) typifies the change of which I am speaking.

It must be said that the admiration felt for America by the Radicals of a hundred years ago was not always well founded. When Cobden, after his triumph in 1846, was presented by his admirers with a considerable sum of money, he invested it all in the Illinois Central Railroad because of his belief in the United States. The railroad went bankrupt, and he lost every penny. It went bankrupt, not for lack of profitable business, and not for lack of skill in the management. Quite the contrary. Bankruptcy was the recognized method of transferring money from simple-minded shareholders to astute directors. But Cobden never grasped this aspect of American big business. And yet to this day Americans believe themselves so naïve as to be liable to be twisted round the little finger of any European who will take the trouble to bamboozle them.

Throughout the period when Radicals inordinately admired America, Conservatives still more inordinately despised it. The Duchess of Cambridge, at a garden party, examined my mother's skirts, saying in a loud voice: "I want to see if they are dirty, because I hear you only associate with dirty Radicals and dirty Americans." Lord Salisbury, the Victorian Prime Minister, saw fit to remind President Cleveland that we owned more of the American continent than the United States did — which displeased Canada almost as much as it displeased the United States. But the days for such insults are past. They depended upon naval supremacy, and when we lost that we had to mend our manners.

The change in the attitude to America of European left-wing opinion is more due to a change in Europe than to a change in America. America in the time of Jefferson believed in democracy and free enterprise, and America believes in them still. Cobden believed in them, and therefore admired America, but left-wing Europeans, nowadays, are Socialists or Communists, and find in America the chief obstacle to the realization of their hopes. There is also another reason for the change of sentiment: people of a rebellious disposition are temperamentally compelled to be against the rich and powerful, and America is more rich and powerful than any other nation. If you praise Sweden to a Communist, he may think you misguided, but will not call you a lackey of capitalism, because Sweden is not great and strong; but if you praise America, there is no limit to the subservience and moral obliquity of which he will suspect you. In the time of Byron and Shelley, both of whom praised America, it was otherwise. America could not threaten anyone, and they imagined it a country of simple farmers imbued with all the virtues of the early Romans. It must be said, however, that Childe Harold never went there.

Although America is opposed to socialism, it would be a mistake to think of the country as unprogressive. Since 1933 immense strides have been taken in social legislation. And in industrial technique — which most Americans think more important than politics — the United States remains the least wedded to tradition and the most receptive to innovations of all the industrial countries with the possible exception of Russia, about which knowledge is unobtainable. In the world of ideas, also, there is a readiness for novelty which is usually absent in Europe. Anyone who has attempted to present a new philosophy to Oxford and the Sorbonne and the universities of America will have been struck by the greater readiness of the Americans to think along unfamiliar lines. And if one could present a new philosophy to Moscow without being liquidated, one would find Russians less open to new ideas than even the most hide-bound old dons in our older universities. All these are facts which left-wing opponents of America fail to recognize.

In international affairs the record of America compares very favorably with that of other Great Powers. There have been, it is true, two short periods of imperialism, one connected with the Mexican War of 1846, the other with the Spanish-American War of 1898, but in each case a change of policy came very soon. In China, where the record of Britain, France, Germany, and Russia is shameful, that of the United States used to be generous and liberal. No territorial concessions were ever demanded, and the Boxer Indemnity money was spent on Chinese education. Since 1945, American policy, both as regards control of atomic power and as regards the Marshall Plan, has been generous and farsighted. Western Union, economic and political, which America urges, is obviously to the interest of Western Europe; in fact, American authorities have shown more awareness of what Western Europe needs than Western Europe itself has shown. True, the United States ought to lower its tariff. But it took Britain thirty-one years after Waterloo to realize a similar need, and it would be unreasonable to expect America to change a traditional policy overnight.

I come now to the main question: How far has the American outlook on life and the world influenced Europe, and how far is it likely to do so?

And first of all: What is the distinctively American outlook? And what, in comparison, is the distinctively European outlook?

Traditionally, the European outlook may be said to be derived from astronomy. When Abraham watched his flocks by night, he observed the stars in their courses: they moved with a majestic regularity utterly remote from human control. When the Lord answered Job out of the whirlwind, He said: "Canst thou bind the sweet influences of Pleiades, or loose the bands of Orion?" The reply was in the negative. Even more relevant is the question: "Knowest thou the ordinances of heaven? Canst thou set the dominion thereof in the earth?" To which Job answered: "Behold, I am vile; what shall I answer thee? I will lay my hand upon my mouth." The conclusion is that man is a feeble creature, to whom only submission and worship are becoming. Pride is insolence, and belief in human power is impiety.

The Greek outlook was similar in this respect. Above even the gods, Necessity or Fate held inexorable sway. The most unforgivable and most swiftly punished of sins was *hubris*, which consisted in the self-assertion of human beings against cosmic laws. This, equally, was a natural outcome of contemplation of the stars.

The Christian religion, Christian art, and Christian literature are deeply impregnated with this spirit of humility. And even among those Europeans who think that they have forgotten religion, it is natural to feel that it is for man to adapt himself to his environment rather than to adapt his environment to himself. Where life is hard, and the medieval tradition is still strong, as in most parts of Europe, this outlook on life still dominates philosophy, literature, and the feelings of ordinary men and women.

In America hardly a trace of this outlook survives. True, the old pious formulas are repeated on Sundays, and are thought, by those who repeat them, to be still believed. But they have lost their grip: they have become only Sunday truths, and during the rest of the week other views prevail. Why bother with the stars? We never see them, because our street lighting is too bright, and in any case they do not have that influence upon human affairs that astrology ascribed to them.

Religion is regarded as a useful influence in human affairs, but its superhuman aspects are forgotten. There is truth in the jest about the newspaper which praised an eminent divine for "the finest prayer ever addressed to a Boston audience." In a modern great city, the works of God are much less noticeable than the works of man. If Job had been reincarnated as an inhabitant of New York, and had been twitted, as the original Job was, with the great size of Leviathan and Behemoth, he would have been unimpressed, and would have replied: "Gee, they ain't half as big as a skyscraper." And as for adaptation to the environment, how lazy and old-fashioned! Compare New York with Manhattan Island as it was when the first white settlers arrived. Is this adaptation of man to his environment? No, it is adaptation of the environment to man. Man is lord of the earth: what he wants, he can get by energy and intelligence. The Soviet government, using an American invention, boasts that it can remove mountains, but not by faith. True, the heavenly bodies remain, but why bother about them? And if, some day, we get tired of the moon, we shall find ways of disintegrating it by radioactive projectiles. To all intents and purposes, God is an adjunct of man, a help in Church work and in procuring victory in man-made wars. The Power that humbled Job out of the whirlwind no longer finds an echo in American mentality.

This attitude to life and the world is inspired by triumphant industrialism, and makes its appeal outside America wherever conditions resemble those in the United States. The country which has a philosophy most similar to that of the United States is Soviet Russia. There, also, there is optimism and energy, there is almost boundless belief in human power, there is determination to regard Nature as providing opportunities rather than obstacles. But in Soviet Russia something remains of ancient piety, imported from the Old

Testament by way of Karl Marx. In heaven the new
synthetic god, Dialectical Materialism, and here below
his vice-regent Stalin, still demand mystical reverence,
since it is man's destiny, willy-nilly, to work out the
the behests of this strange Hegelian-Hebraic Deity.
But perhaps this lingering remnant of earlier philoso-
phies will only survive as long as Russia remains poor;
given prosperity, the new religion might lose influence
in Russia as completely as the old religion has in the
United States.

From the highest flights of philosophy to the silliest
movie, the distinctive feature of American thought and
feeling is a determination to have done with the notion
of "fact." We used to think it a good thing if our beliefs were "true," and we imagined that "truth" consisted in correspondence with "fact." If you believe
(say) that Edinburgh is north of London, you believe
truly, because of a geographical fact which is quite
independent of your belief. And so we thought it our
duty to recognize "facts," even if they were unpleasant.
Not so, says pragmatism, which is the typical American philosophy: there are no "facts" that have to be
passively acknowledged, and "truth" is a mistaken
concept. Dewey, the leading philosopher of America,
replaces "truth" by "warranted assertibility." This is
arrived at, not by merely observing the environment,
but by an interaction with it which continues until it
has been so modified as to become acceptable to us.

For passive "truth" he substitutes active "inquiry," which he says, "is concerned with objective transformations of objective subject-matter."

"Inquiry," according to this view, is like extracting a metal from the ore, or turning raw cotton into cloth. The raw material offered to our senses is not assimilable, and we put it through a process until, like an invalid food, it becomes easy to digest. A belief only has "warranted assertibility" when the consequences of holding the belief are satisfactory. Some governments have not been slow to realize that the police can decide what beliefs shall have "satisfactory" consequences. In old days, a belief might be "true" even if the Government frowned on it; now it cannot have "warranted assertibility" if the police object to it — unless those who hold it are strong enough to promote a successful revolution.

The political consequences of such a philosophy have been worked out with ruthless logic in George Orwell's book, *Nineteen Eighty-Four*. But none of his gloomy forecasts will have "warranted assertibility" if they turn out to be "true," for anyone who adheres to them after they have been realized will be liquidated, and therefore the consequences of adhering to them will not be "satisfactory."

The artistic consequences of the refusal to admit "facts" are equally bad. From pragmatism to the movies is not such a far cry as might be thought. I

believe almost every European would agree that the
English, the French, the Germans, and the Russians
of some twenty years ago, all produced artistically better movies than those emanating from Hollywood.
When we see an American film we know beforehand
that virtue will be rewarded, that crime will be shown
not to pay, and that the heroine, always faultlessly
dressed in spite of incredible tribulations, will emerge
happily to life-long bliss with the hero. If you object,
"But this is a sugary fairy tale only fit for children,"
producers and American public alike will be simply
puzzled, since the object is not to produce something
that corresponds to fact, but something that makes
you happy by corresponding to daydreams.

It is natural that, by contrast, some of the best
American novelists are savage, cynical, and pessimis-
tic. I wish they had as large a public as is enjoyed by
the movies — though, if they had, they would no doubt
become less savage and less cynical.

The lack of aesthetic sense produced by an excessive
preoccupation with utility shows also in the matter of
speech. Educated people throughout Europe, and
peasants on the Continent and in Scotland and Ireland,
have a certain beauty of diction: language is not
merely a means of communication, but a vehicle for
expressing the emotions of joy or sorrow, love or hate,
that are the material of poetry. Words, many of them,
have beauty; they have a history, and we are, each in

our own day, responsible for handing on an unimpaired tradition in diction and enunciation. It is rare to find this feeling among Americans. If you make your meaning clear, what more can be desired? Accordingly their vocabulary is small, and sounds which should be distinguished are blurred. The only good thing about the American language is the slang. Fortunately, it is just this that the English are most disposed to copy.

I console myself with the reflection that French, now such a beautiful language, was in origin the argot of uneducated Roman soldiers. Perhaps in fifteen hundred years American will become equally admirable.

But I have been dwelling too much upon what seems to me regrettable in the American outlook. There is another side, and one which it is very important that Europe should appreciate.

The American outlook is the result of inhabiting a large country, not yet over-populated, with immense natural resources, and with greater wealth and less poverty than any of the old countries of Europe and Asia. A young American can be adventurous without folly; he does not need, to nearly the same extent as a European, to force himself into acquiescence with a narrow groove and a career that can be foreseen with dreary accuracy. The hopefulness and enterprise that circumstances permit increase the success that is achieved beyond what would be possible for men of a different temperament. Obstacles, it is felt, exist to be overcome, and therefore they are overcome. All this is admirable. It existed in Elizabethan England, and to a lesser degree in Victorian England. It is now lost to us, but I hope not forever. A little more of this American spirit would do us far more good than any amount of austerity unrelieved by hope.

Britain, and Western Europe generally, have new and very difficult problems to face. When we are lectured by optimistic Americans we are apt to feel the kind of annoyance that a suffering patient feels with a doctor whose bedside manner is unduly cheerful; we cannot resist the reflection that it is easy to be cheerful about other people's troubles. But we shall not solve our problems unless we believe them soluble, and we shall not solve them without a certain buoyancy of spirit, of which, at the moment, America and Russia share the monopoly. Austerity is unavoidable at present, but it should resemble the frugality of a young man determined to succeed, not the parsimony of an old man who fears to lose the last remnant of his former fortune. Fear has led us to lay too much emphasis on safety, and too little on enterprise. Without risk, nothing can be achieved. In this respect, I welcome the impact of America, and I only wish that Western Europe were more receptive.

A great deal of nonsense is talked about American so-called "materialism" and what its detractors call "bathroom civilization." I do not think Americans are in any degree more "materialistic," in the popular sense of that word, than people of other nations. We think they worship the "almighty dollar" because they succeed in getting it. But a needy aristocrat or a French peasant will do things for the sake of money that shock every decent American. Very few Americans marry from mercenary motives. A willingness to sacrifice income for idealistic reasons is at least as common in America as in England. I think the belief that Americans are fonder of money than we are is mainly inspired by envy. It is true that, where there is no recognized aristocracy, wealth is the chief means of winning general respect. But where aristocracy has prevailed, individual aristocrats have been respected because most aristocrats were rich. Now that this is no longer true in Europe, American standards, as regards snobbery, are rapidly coming to be accepted.

As for "bathroom civilization," it is altogether to the good, unless it is thought to be all-sufficient. Every traveler owes a debt of gratitude to American tourists for the improvement in hotels that has been brought about by their grumbling. The love of "gadgets," for which we are inclined to make fun of Americans, ought not to be decried. An American middle-class housewife, compelled, like an English housewife, to do her own cooking, does it with far less labor than is required in most English kitchens. The habit of keeping food in the refrigerator is wholly to be commended from the point of view of health. The more we copy America in these respects, the better.

It is not only in utilitarian ways that the best Americans are admirable. What could be less utilitarian than the study of extra-galactic nebulae? Yet here far and away the best work has been done in America. True, the reason is that America has the best telescopes, and has them because there are very rich men in America who think this a good way of spending some of their money. But they would not think so if they and their public were as earth-bound as is often supposed by Europeans.

There is one aspect of American life which I have not yet touched on, and which I think wholly undesirable — I mean, the tyranny of the herd. Eccentricity is frowned upon, and unusual opinions bring social penalties upon those who hold them. At the present day, people suspected of even the slightest sympathy with communism are exposed to a kind of ostracism which would be absurd if it were not tragic. Atomic physicists maintain that the inquisition instigated by Congress is seriously impeding important war work. After the first World War, there was a terrible persecution of Radicals; the case of Sacco and Vanzetti made the most stir, but there were many others only slightly less shocking. The guilt lies with the general public, which is intolerant to a degree that must astonish any

Englishman. It has nothing to do with industrialism; indeed, it is worst in purely rural communities. It is not a new thing; it was noted by Tocqueville in his book on American democracy; it was rampant in the time of Washington; and it goes back to the early Puritan colonies of the seventeenth century. It is, I think, the worst feature of America. I earnestly hope that fear of Russia will not cause us to imitate it.

The shift in world power, which is largely, though not wholly, the result of the two wars, is bound to bring with it, as such shifts always do, cultural changes of great importance. From the sixteenth century onward, Europe increasingly dominated the world, from a cultural no less than a military point of view. Now that domination is lost; the inheritance is divided between Russia and America. The culture of America is closely akin to our own, and adaptation can be easy and painless. The culture of Russia, on the other hand, is profoundly alien: partly Byzantine, partly Mongol, only quite superficially European. Only appalling suffering could force us into the Russian mold. It is therefore the part of wisdom to facilitate co-operation with America, cultural as well as political and economic.

In some respects, it must be admitted, adoption of American standards, in so far as it occurs, is likely to be harmful. Aesthetic standards, except in architecture, will probably be lowered. There will be less respect for art and learning, and more for the forceful "executive." The movement towards socialism will be retarded — but whether that is to be regarded as a gain or a loss is a controversial question.

On the other side, however, are to be set gains which far outweigh possible losses. Our continued existence as free nations is only capable of being maintained by co-operation with America. Our tired and disillusioned communities, which, as independent separate entities, would be condemned to live on memories under the oppression of poverty and danger, can, in conjunction with America, recover a status less different from that to which they have been accustomed in recent centuries. Above all things, European culture, if it is to remain vital, needs hope and imaginative vision. These things are common in America, as they were in Victorian England. If we can recover them by contact with Americans, there is every possibility of a future no less glorious and no less happy than our past.

2

THE LESSON OF THE PUPIL

John Lehmann

JOHN LEHMANN

The Lesson of the Pupil

It has often struck me that the opening scene of Henry James's story, "The Lesson of the Master," forms an attractively symbolic representation of James's own attitude towards European culture — his attitude as a young man, as young as his hero Paul Overt, who sees Summersoft for the first time on "a splendid Sunday in June." "The long bright gallery," "the immense lawn" and "the great trees" seen from the top of the circular sweep of the steps, all "went together and spoke in one voice — a rich English voice of the early part of the eighteenth century"; and in the midst of this ideal setting of mellow centuries and civilized taste, somewhere in the distinguished company dispersed among the avenues and shrubberies, was the "high literary figure," the legendary master at whose shrine Paul Overt had come to worship.

I was brought up in a house where the works of Hawthorne and Emerson and Poe were prominent on the shelves beside Dickens and the Brontës and Tennyson, and all that I absorbed from the talk of our parents, and our American relations and friends when they came on their summer visits, led me to regard these New England writers of the nineteenth century as the true and dignified literature of America, indeed as the only literature there was in that continent, with its roots deep in our own English literature, its sunflower face turned forever towards Europe. That was not, of course, by any means an entirely true picture, and I have since come to understand that the American impulse towards a self-consciously American literature started long before the opening of the present century. Nevertheless, even Walt Whitman, so aggressively democratic in the American sense, so eager to announce a "Placard 'removed' and 'to let' " on Parnassus and the arrival of a new transatlantic muse "installed amid the kitchenware," even Walt Whitman formed his rhythms on those of our English seventeenth century prose and used a high-poetic language that had nothing specifically American about it.

What a revolution there has been since that day. Paul Overt was not, in the story, an American, but if we take him as a figure for James himself arriving on the scene of European culture, we can see that it is the pupil now who is busy teaching the master, and it is to Henry James that the descendants of Summersoft's "high literary figure" look so ardently to reveal the inspiration and the way. What a strange irony of history that Europe should search for its lost secrets in an American mirror — only fifty years later. And it is not only Henry James that enjoys this high place: Herman Melville, too, has grown to a figure of supreme significance on this side of the Atlantic; and a younger expatriate from the eastern American seaboard, T. S. Eliot, is now revered as England's greatest poet — perhaps, since the death of Paul Valéry, Europe's greatest poet. Nor is it in England alone that Melville's cult has flourished: in France, Germany, Italy in recent years the fame of *Moby Dick* and *Billy Budd* has spread rapidly, new translations have been made, articles multiplied in all the literary reviews.

Yet neither Henry James, nor Herman Melville, nor T. S. Eliot can be called representative of a new, specifically American literature. The traditional European influences that molded them are too clear, too well known to need pointing out again; and no word of the tough slang of Manhattan or Chicago ever irrupted into their polished lines or paragraphs. They take their place without awkwardness or shocking contrast beside the classic New England authors I fingered in the library shelves in my boyhood — though perhaps I should exclude *Sweeney Agonistes* from this generalization. "I'm going to be surprisingly better," says Overt to the Master in their first interview; and the Master replies: "I see that, and it's what fetches me. I don't see so much else — as one looks about — that's going to be surprisingly better. They're going to be consistently worse — most of the things. It's so much easier to be worse — heaven knows I've found it so. I'm not in a great glow, you know, about what's breaking out all over the place."

One of the things that have broken out since then is Mr. Ernest Hemingway; and one cannot believe that the Master would have thought him "surprisingly better." And yet I can remember that many years ago, when I was all keenness to begin writing myself, a distinguished literary figure in London told me that I must read Hemingway, that I should be hopelessly out of step with the times unless I read Hemingway. So to drunken Brett I went, whoring her way through the fiestas in Spain, and tried to forget Summersoft and the "long bright gallery."

The distinguished literary figure was, of course, right to give me this advice. For the American realists who appeared in the twenties and thirties, with Hemingway at their head, had a revolutionary effect on the writing of fiction, on both sides of the Atlantic. There is a passage in Cyril Connolly's *Enemies of Promise*, in his famous discussion on the Mandarin and Vernacular styles, where he says: "The outstanding writer of the new vernacular is Hemingway, and he was aided by the talkies as were realists a generation before by journalism. The talking picture," Connolly goes on, "popularized the vocabulary with which Hemingway wrote and enabled him to use slang words in the knowledge that they were getting every day less obscure; he surf-rode into fame on the wave of American popular culture." Cyril Connolly hit the nail on the head: the modern American colloquial washed over Britain with the force of a tidal wave because of the tremendous power of the cinema, and Hemingway suddenly appeared as the most brilliant talker in this new style. No wonder his popularity became a craze; no wonder his style was imitated everywhere; and equally no wonder, in view of its "dumb ox" limitations, it rapidly degenerated in the hands of its imitators into an artificial trick for simulating toughness.

The most popular literature today, the cheap paper books that sell in hundreds of thousands — and millions — often more under the counter than over it, the lurid sex and crime stories that pass from hand to hand in soldiers' barracks and are stuffed under pillows in seamen's bunks, are all written in a bastard Hemingwayese that seems to be remorselessly driving out the old, native English, popular slang. Lord Russell observed, in Chapter 1, that "the only good thing about the American language is the slang." He is right; but it is certainly not the stereotyped slang of such books, designed to eliminate the use of the mind, but rather that fertile slang, vivid in unexpected wit and image, that almost any American will use — will, rather, *create* — when stimulated by fresh experiences or contacts. In that indeed is an Elizabethan touch, a life-giving touch, and it is strange how far it is to seek in the work of the popular realists.

It would be wrong, however, to conclude that the influence of Hemingway and his fellow American realists has only been debasing. On the contrary, one has only to read a story by V. S. Pritchett or Christopher Isherwood, to see how the most skillful writers of a younger generation over here have assimilated his innovations to add fresh brilliance to their own writing. Above all, in the modern English novel, the mark of Hemingway is seen at its clearest, I believe, in the increasing use of dialogue — dialogue taking over much of the function that comparatively lengthy descriptive and reflective passages used to have — and in the quickened pace that this naturally brings with it.

In Europe also, since the war, the new American realists have had a profound effect. Indeed it has been one of the more curious phenomena of the forties, how a rage developed in France and Italy for Hemingway, Steinbeck, Dos Passos, Caldwell and other writers of their ilk. We in Britain meanwhile have been thinking of them as belonging to a rather outmoded phase of literary development. The flame was undoubtedly fanned by the movies, by the penetration of the American film far beyond the Anglo-Saxon world; but the real appeal, I cannot help thinking, was primarily political. Not merely, or even mainly, that the thoughts of all the German-oppressed peoples turned towards America in the last years of the war; but rather that these American realists seemed to have solved certain problems of *democratic* writing that were vexing the minds of the intellectuals in the left-wing resistance coalitions that were forming underground as the German hold weakened. The raw exposure of the living and working conditions of the American masses, the sense of justice outraged, the violence of class and racial conflict displayed, the vernacular vigor of speech — all these elements had an intoxicating appeal to intellectuals living in a gale that seemed likely to uproot the old social order after it had scattered the foreign invaders like autumn leaves. Many of the new Italian writers, such as Vittorini, Berto, Pratolini, are obviously deeply indebted to the generation of Hemingway and Steinbeck. Nothing is more fascinating than to compare the pre-war technique of Jean-Paul Sartre in *La Nausée* with his Dos Passos-soaked technique in the postwar *Chemins de la Liberté*. And the files of almost any European literary magazine of the last five years will reveal contribution after contribution devoted to the transatlantic realist Parnassus, critiques and translations and interviews galore.

To an exhausted Europe, of course, it is the surface vigor, the air of boyish exuberance about modern American writing that seems so invigorating. Dr. Leslie Hotson, that brilliant and indefatigable unraveler of Shakespearean riddles, said recently:

In our day, we talk a great deal, and very enthusiastically, too, about the Elizabethan Age. With us Americans it is a delighted and proud ancestor-worship. But we are human, and fall into the facile subjective error of praising Shakespeare's age only for the qualities we fancy in ourselves. Thus, we extol the Elizabethan youthful vitality, the nation's zest in pioneering enterprise; we share its pride in prosperity and new-found importance in the family of nations, and approve the opportunities for initiative and ambition that resulted in the rise of the middle class. . . .

Dr. Hotson goes on to point out that this simplified view cannot stand up to expert examination; that though the educated Elizabethans may have comprised a very small class, their culture was far deeper, their learning more thorough, their wits nimbler than their American dittos of today; that religion was a profound reality to them; and that their world was more spacious "because their morality had little room for hypocrisy," and "because their life embraced unafraid traffic with painful emotions, that is, with passions." In sum, the Elizabethans, Dr. Hotson is saying, not only believed that life had a meaning, a center, but also knew a technique to cope with its worst buffets. And he implies, I think, that the modern American has not got this. He implies that, because the gadget-civilization he has so brilliantly perfected lacks a proper spiritual basis, much of his vigor and inventiveness proves spurious and hollow on closer examination.

Something, in fact, has gone wrong with Walt Whitman's noble vision, in the middle of the last century, of the great new democratic America inspired by brotherhood and love and religion.

Does the toast he raised taste bitter now? It is a strange fact that, though some of the American writers of the last two generations may have followed too literally his challenge to "report all heroism from an American point of view," what strikes one about them as a whole is the astonishing prevalence of a hatred for, a revulsion against, their own civilization. And this, all too often, produces an underlying cynicism and despair. This spiritual emptiness is surely the drop of poison in the cup, the corrupting influence that American literature today, in the time of its great vogue, may have on European literature. The Americans express it with great power — they never do anything by halves — and in that lies the danger. In the finest writers it is, of course, deeply moving, because they are conscious of what is lost; but in the lesser writers it leads to that literature of phony values, or without values at all, that is the stuff of best-sellers and the meat of the movie-makers.

Personally, I take the view that there is growing up in America a new generation of writers who are determined to find positive values, not in the exploded myth of endless industrial progress, but in the heart and soul of man. Mr. Evelyn Waugh wrote an article recently on "The American Epoch in the Catholic Church." In it he said:

Unhappily "Americanism" has come to mean for most of the world what a few, very vociferous, far from typical Americans wish to make it. The people of other continents look to America half in hope and half in alarm. They see that their own future is inextricably involved with it, and their judgment is based on what they see in the cinema, what they read in the popular magazines, what they learn from the loudest advertiser. Gratitude for the enormous material benefits received is tempered with distaste for what they believe is the spiritual poverty of the benefactor. It is only when one travels in America that one realizes that most Americans either share this distaste or are genuinely unaware of the kind of false impression which interested parties have conspired to spread.

Now I would wholeheartedly agree with him that the more Americans one gets to know, and the more one travels in America, the more one is impressed by the warmth of heart, the idealism and the Christian feeling of the American people; even if, when it comes to business and business morality, they sometimes seem to suffer from a kind of schizophrenia. I am not, as a Protestant of Puritan ancestry, prepared to go all the way with Mr. Waugh when he further asserts that in American Christianity it is pre-eminently Catholicism that is the redeeming part; but I do hold that the forces representing something other than cynicism and reckless materialism are too strong not to make themselves felt one day, in literature too. It will be a good day for

Europe when that happens. Perhaps the parallel forces in Europe may help it to happen, because cultural influence between the two continents is far from a one-way traffic even today. One cannot but be impressed by the respect in which leading British writers are held in America — by the enormous success which, for instance, Elizabeth Bowen, Graham Greene and Henry Green have had there in the last few years. And after all, the culture which produced an Emerson, a Whitman, a Melville, may produce as great a writer and as great a soul again. Then indeed Whitman's famous lines will have come true:

I conned old times,
I sat studying at the feet of the great masters,
Now if eligible o that the great masters might return and study
   me.

3

"LOOK HOMEWARD, ANGEL"

Sean O'Faolain

After receiving M.A. degrees from the National University of Ireland and Harvard, SEAN O'FAOLAIN lectured for a year at Boston College. He has subsequently written several biographies, plays, and other books, the most recent being *Summer in Italy*.

SEAN O'FAOLAIN

"Look Homeward, Angel"

When I think of the United States influencing
Europe, the first question I ask myself is — what is the
United States? And the first thing I think about then
is that the language spoken in the United States is a
European language. And the second thing I think of
is that the United States is, with the exception of the
Negroes and the Indians, entirely composed of European emigrants and their descendants. The influence
of the U.S.A. on Europe is the influence of a grandchild
on his grandfather. This possibly will, if all goes well,
be known in time as the Aeneas-Anchises complex in
grateful commemoration of the bravery, or obstinacy,
of Aeneas in carrying his purblind sire out of the
crumbling city of Troy.

In America this relationship is honored every
twenty-second of September on Forefathers' Day.
Well, I am afraid they let off many more rockets on
June 17th to honor the battle of Bunker Hill, on which
date pious Aeneas is believed to have begun a successful war of independence to get rid of the old man on

37

his back. And just to remind ourselves forever of the complexity of these matters, we may recollect that Bunker Hill is in Boston, and that some Irish-Americans made a great junketing on that day, being under a confused impression that the English were defeated at Bunker Hill — which they were not — and that it was the Irish who won the battle, which is true only in the sense that General Howe was a member of the Irish peerage.

James Joyce said to Yeats on a memorable occasion, "I am afraid, sire, you are too old to be influenced by me." Our American grandnephews have had no such inhibitions of genius, and least of all Patrick, the new transatlantic patrician. Now here I want to talk only about Patrick, because what he thinks about Europe is a microcosm of what all Americans, descended from Polish, French, English, Italian, German, Spanish, Scandinavian, or Central European grandsires think about Europe. To Patrick, Europe is, of course, primarily and emotionally Ireland. It may even be Balahadareen's one main street, just as to an Italian Europe may mean a girl in Lucca, or the pub in Fontamara.

Now the first thing we observe about these emigrants is that the farther away each of them goes from the old land, the more he loves it. The nearer he comes to it the cooler he gets. His nostalgia reminds us of George Eliot's comment about charity — that its force is in inverse ratio to its distance from its object. We

know this very well in Ireland, or we used to know it
very well, when emigration was at its height. For few
figures were so familiar to us as the returned "Yank,"
as we used to call him, always telling us stay-at-homes
what slow-coaches we were, and how we wasted our
time, and how much better everything is done "over
there." We used to listen respectfully and pay not
the slightest heed, because we understood very well
what was biting the poor fellow. He'd been pulled
back to Ireland by those very things that he derided
when he got home, and he derided them because, if
he didn't, he might never return to the land of milk
and honey. One meets Italians in Italy who do exactly
the same thing. They return to Italy, full of desire.
They leave it, full of derision. All emigrants suffer this
neurosis of maladjustment. Their relationship with the
old country is as uneasy as all family relationships are.
And there's no place like home when you are not living
in it.

The Irish-American's neurosis is one of loss, and of
fear resulting from loss. You see, in Ireland an Irishman is easygoing, garrulous, jocose, indifferent to the
clock, or food, and serious about a lot of unserious
things, such as sport. And he's all this because he lives
in a country with a comfortable tempo and only the
mildest of challenges, and in the security of a society
which is an interweaving of protective, personal and
family relationships.

Now, land that same man in Chicago or New York, and what happens? He is uprooted, isolated, torn from all those cushioning family connections, and he at once becomes hard-working, ambitious, and ruthless. And yet he will think back with the fondest affection to the country whose habits he has so effectively discarded. He glorifies it; he magnifies it so much, so extravagantly so, with such nostalgia that it is largely a chimera that he loves now, a phantasm of his own imagination. If the old land fails to live up to his image of it, even, let's say, in literature, how angry he is. No wonder that the Irish in America rioted over Synge's *Playboy of the Western World*, and O'Casey's *The Plough and the Stars*. Evelyn Waugh told us the other day that he saw the Italian film *Paesan* in a Chicago cinema, with a largely Sicilian audience, and that the Italians laughed to scorn the sequence about the poor friars. And then, one feels, the poor devils went off to the saloon and got maudlin, singing Sicilian love-songs. The whole thing is a mixture of love and longing and emotional unrest and, perhaps, a spot of inferiority complex.

It may be an unkind way to say it, but it is not untrue. The Irishman in America is the fox that has lost his tail, and so he wears a tail, bigger and bushier and more flamboyant than any Irish tail that ever was, and woe to the man who treads on it. Are all Americans more European than the Europeans? When they're cross with Europe, may it not be less because Europe is letting down America than because Europe is letting down Europe, or their idea of it, their precious dream-world? It is certainly true that the Irish in America have always wanted Ireland to be far more Irish than Ireland ever wanted to be, or more Irish in a way that we never want it to be.

Sometimes they send us accounts of things like a St. Patrick's Day in South Boston that make us squirm with embarrassment. Men on white horses, carrying lances, dressed in white buckskins, in green swallow-tailed coats, and black sombreros with white ostrich feathers; hosts of girls dressed as little Green Riding Hoods. Well, how could we ever live up to so magnificent a fantasy? We feel ashamed at being so commonplace and so unromantic. Yeats said:

> Romantic Ireland's dead and gone.
> 'Tis with O'Leary in the grave.

It's with O'Leary in Chicago.

All in all the emigrant sets a high standard, and not always a feasible or realistic standard for the home country. Now the interesting thing is, if this dream of the old country is the Irish-American's poetry, or his myth, he has the extraordinary power of keeping it untarnished by his own experience. Whatever he's observed, or experienced, or learned in the United

States, isn't permitted to be related to Ireland. For example, it is only American intellectuals who apply to Europe that principle of the unification of states and peoples which the United States exemplifies for every one of its citizens. And these intellectuals are generally men of established stock, whose affiliations with Europe are old, faint, perhaps boiled down to something as slight as a silver spoon that came over with the *Mayflower*.

The Irish-American, on the other hand, who would have laughed yesterday at the idea of Home Rule for Massachusetts, whose father may have fought for the Union, was all for Home Rule for Ireland. Today he'd laugh at the idea of a self-contained, self-sufficient Alabama. But he's all for Ireland building up self-sufficiency behind tariff walls. Tomorrow if anybody could seriously propose the obliteration of all national languages in Europe in favor of one European language, he'd be up in arms in defense of the old country's language, even though he mightn't be able to speak a word of it himself. And never, never would he tolerate the idea of a United States of Great Britain and Ireland, with local legislatures and one central federal Parliament. In this respect the Old World and the New World are a universe apart. And so, it doesn't in the least trouble Patrick if the old country remains old-fashioned and conservative, nationalistic, even chauvinistic, traditional, simple, even backward. As he drives through it in his high-powered automobile on his return visits he loves to see the donkey and cart trundling to the creamery. He regrets the passing of the old thatched roofs; he drinks in the smell of the burning peat, which everybody else would gladly exchange for good English coal. He's a bit of a swindler in this, for he will simultaneously demand first-class motoring roads and first-class hotels at low rates, with bedside telephone and private bath; and, as I've said, he will complain on a turn of the wrist that the whole darn place is slow and inefficient whenever he wants to revert to the role of the emigrant who made good.

Well, evidently values are clashing here. He's of no help to us in our own little efforts to decide on our own values. As Pat the patrician leans out of his Chrysler and praises the old ways, Pat the plebeian enviously eyes the car, and goes away full of cynicism and dissatisfaction. Look homeward, angel? Rather enter Asmodeus bearing a fresh muddle.

Now, another thing. The illiberal tendencies of the Irish in America are one of the strangest things about their latter-day development. Just as they were unsympathetic to the Negroes in the nineteenth century, they have been found unsympathetic to the Jews in our own time. It's only a couple of years since anti-Semitic trouble in Boston was traced to the Irish. We are familiar with the activities of Father Coughlin; we

were recently shocked by the rigorous anti-Protestant-
ism of Father Feeney. This doesn't help liberal
thought in Ireland, which in any case has a hard enough
furrow to plow and could do with all the help that it
might have expected from the Land of the Free. But
there's a long and complex tradition behind this Irish-
American illiberalism. No race, bar the Negroes, were
in the bad days so brutally exploited, no race so cruelly
taught the lesson of the survival of the toughest. It is
only right to say that intelligent opinion at home
roundly condemns this sort of thing. But it must do
harm. And it does.

This must bring me to another plane — where the
interplay of the Old World and the New World is much
more harmonious. I mean the plane of religion. The
Catholic Church at home and in the United States is a
firm handclasp across the sea; one in tone, one in tradition and one in technique. Indeed, allowing, to be
sure, for local variations, Catholicism in the United
States could be thoroughly and conveniently studied
on Irish soil. The Catholic Church in America is, as
we know, strongly influenced by the Irish. It ought to
be, since it was largely built by the Irish, with much
the same hearty vigor and muscular energy that they
put into building the roaring U.P. trail. Now at all
times the Irish Catholic immigrant in America has
been strongly right-wing. There was hardly a single
radical, revolutionary, or reformatory movement

throughout the nineteenth century that he didn't condemn, often even Irish ones. He opposed Lincoln; he favored Negro slavery; he persistently opposed social reform; he upheld the Democratic Party in the South. The Irish-American immigrant's reasons for this, however, whether they were or were not backward, were and still are soundly based on two strong principles: respect for authority, and a mistrust of the secular state, sometimes called the pagan state. Occasionally these principles collided. In our time, for instance, the Catholic Irish in America jettisoned authority to oppose the secular reform of Prohibition, just as in the nineteenth century they'd have nothing to do with temperance reform. Both of these things were to them the secular state trying to bring a very dubious heaven to earth. Their attitude was that the only institution fit to reform anything or anybody was the Church. Another seeming contradiction was their behavior in the Civil War, because having for years supported the South and slavery, the Irishman and the Yankee fought side by side for the Union and for lawfully appointed government. Once the final constitutional issue was knit, in both cases they supported tradition. If they had to choose between a religion and a secular tradition, in a crisis they chose what they considered the more important tradition.

And so today nothing is more natural, being traditional, than that the priests, who flock back to Ireland in the summer months (some of them emigrants, some of them sons or grandsons of emigrants), should bring with them, and be delighted to find before them, a rooted anti-radicalism, traditionalism, and conservatism. We fete them proudly and we welcome them warmly, and they repay the compliment by giving us the impression that if it weren't for Ireland at home and Ireland abroad, Christianity would founder, and secularism, by which they mean communism, would rule the world. It disturbs nobody that there are not from one end of Ireland to the other more than about a dozen Communists — if that. I never have met even one. On the contrary it goes to prove the main contention.

Here old Ireland never lets Irish-America down. Here the ideas of the old country and of the New World stiffen one another in a common front of not merely rigid, but truculent opposition to anything remotely savoring of statism. Even socialism or left-wing liberalism is enough to make that long, Irish upper lip get a bit longer still. The fact is that Irishmen may be rebels, but they are not reformers. Like all peoples of peasant, Catholic stock, they're firm believers in God's established ways on earth, and the imperfectibility of human nature; and after all, if an Irish emigrant were to believe in the perfectibility of human nature, he wouldn't be what he is, but an eighteenth-century Deist. It must be made quite clear however that he does believe in the perfectibility of private property.

The upshot of all this is that we tend to think of the American as a modern product. Half of him is. The other half is ruled by atavisms of the nineteenth century. He may think, whether he be a Pole, or an Irishman, or a Greek, or an Armenian, that he's thinking to the tick of his electric clock. He is feeling by the throb of his grandfather's heart. In a word, all those nostalgic emigrants are dyed-in-the-wool Tories. We must never suspect these great masses of homeward-dreaming angels of wishing to Americanize Europe. That's the last thing they want to do. But they are frighteningly sentimental about it, and wildly ignorant of Europe as it now is, and their attitude to it is fissured and bedeviled by their own unresolved contradictions. We could never estimate American opinion about Europe by their opinion. They haven't got an opinion, merely a muddled set of feelings. As for their influence on Europe, the best one can say of it is that it is, however sentimentally and unintellectually, strongly on the side of traditionalism and conservatism. The worst one can say of it is that it is stubbornly and bitterly unmalleable and reactionary. One may not believe that these backward-looking masses formulate policy, but one may well believe that they are often a trying problem for those who do — on both sides of the Atlantic.

4

HOLLYWOOD: AMERICA'S VOICE

J. E. Morpurgo

J. E. MORPURGO was educated in England at Christ's Hospital, and in Virginia at the College of William and Mary. Both as a writer and as a publisher, he has given much attention to American history and literature. *The New York Times* has referred to him as an "Anglo-American."

J. E. Morpurgo

Hollywood: America's Voice

In the first chapter, Bertrand Russell spoke of Europeans with pretensions to culture who are apt to remember Hollywood with a sniff. I share Lord Russell's distaste for all those who choose to regard Hollywood either as the zenith or as the totality of American cultural achievement, and yet I am doomed to serve with them for it is my task here to discuss Hollywood's influence on Europe.

Millions who have never left Britain know the United States. To the film-going public the appearance of things American is as familiar as Sauchiehall Street to the Glaswegian or the lights of Piccadilly to the Londoner. Visually America is the best-known country in the world. The towering New York skyline, the white clapboard houses of New England, the Golden Gate, the magnificence of the Rockies; these pictures have become, through cinematic repetition, part of the Englishman's pictorial equipment, and with Hollywood's aid he has developed an intimate acquaintance with such peculiarly American institutions

as the drugstore, the tourist-cabin, the fraternity house
and the railroad depot.

Yet we do not know America. We know less about
America than we know about any other world power
and we misconstrue the little that we do know. For
as we accept the obviously realistic Hollywood ex-
teriors, so also do we imagine that we have seen what
lies behind, and by the falsifying persuasions of Hollywood are led to believe that we understand the spirit
as well as the physical appearance of the United States.

Hollywood — an excellent entertainer — is not
merely an entertainer. To some people more than
to others, but to all people in some degree, the film
has taken the place of the older arts. Unfortunately, if
it is true that there has never been an art equal to the
art of the cinema for its universal appeal, it is also true
that only in this art has American effort been comparable to a similar effort by Europe.

We who admire American achievement may prefer
to roll out the more glorious names — Jonathan Edwards, Dos Passos, Franklin, and Millikan — but their
influence was either essentially confined to their coun-
trymen or else it was qualitative, touching only upon
the thought of their equals, their fellow practitioners
and their few admirers. But the influence of Hollywood is international and quantitative. Herman Melville in his essay on Hawthorne twisted, to suit his
own chauvinism, an arrogant phrase of Sydney Smith's:

HOLLYWOOD: AMERICA'S VOICE   53

"The day will come," Melville wrote, "when you shall say, who reads a book by an Englishman who is a modern?" The day has come when the literary, the unliterary, and the illiterate are all sitting in on the work of Americans. In the cinema, for the first time, America works in a medium in which her people are both unquestionably powerful and generally more competent than the people of other nations. It is not altogether surprising that Europeans are inclined to take as typical of America, this, the one art in which American achievement is supreme.

The rise of Hollywood has come about at a time when America must take over from Europe some of Europe's centuries-old duties. The will to leadership undoubtedly exists in the American people. They have the power, the ideals, and the intellectual force. They have — in Hollywood — a vehicle by which to convey their own purposes and their own faith. But Hollywood has represented American weakness instead of American strength. It has revealed America, as she is in part: the heir to European decay. It has not shown the other America: the heir to Europe's old strength who has taken on a vigor that is all her own. Hollywood has given back to Europe Europe's own mental vices, and has encouraged them, both in Europeans and in the Americans themselves.

Almost from the day when the United States was founded America has been involved in a conflict between practice and ideal, between utility and history, confidence and thought, orthodoxy and rebellion. The shallower, the lazier, the more comfortable way has, of recent years, been nearer to the surface; the pioneer spirit that looked upon all problems, both physical and intellectual, as obstacles to be overcome by the individual, has, of recent years, been close to extinction. This individual determination could have helped Europe, but Hollywood has played up the easier paths, has emphasized the sybaritic aspects of the American character. It has perpetuated in the American people their love of mass satisfaction and has helped Europe to the same easy enthusiasm.

Looking back with the bright superiority of the historian it is possible to see that European exhaustion is not merely the product of two wars, but that the process was already beginning at the end of the eighteenth century; that already then cracks were appearing in European civilization. It was then that utilitarian motives began to take the place of the lonely processes of creative thought. It was then that productive activity began to be diverted into technical fields, that mass education began to be regarded as alternative and superior to individual effort and personal quest. Europe was then already losing hope.

At about the same time America, still a nonentity among the nations, offered something to Europe that might have rejuvenated the Old World: America pre-

sented to the world in practical terms the proposition
that had for long lingered unspoken in man's mind, the
proposition that all men are created equal. To some
extent Europe took America's offer. Uneasily, sometimes with success and often with shattering failure,
Europe tried to follow the American call. The spirit
of '76 went to the heads of Europeans and warmed
them to the necessity for equality. The leaders of
nineteenth-century reform sang "Yankee Doodle
Dandy" in their hearts, and the American Revolution
was their inspiration as much as the French. More
perhaps: for the American Revolution was successful
and efficient; America was a democracy — a working
democracy, or so it seemed to the liberals; the American example could be followed and a pattern of work-
able democracy created.

Throughout the nineteenth century Europe struggled
to make law from natural law, but, when the process
was still far from complete, the two wars made it
essential that Europe should once more listen to the
call of Jefferson, that America should come back to the
aid of Europe. Unfortunately, comfortable America
had turned a deaf ear to her own founders; the first
deserters from the principles of the American Revolution were the Americans themselves. America, the
model for Europe, America, the efficient democracy,
was not working. Success had brought ease, ease had
brought laziness, and the principle that all men were

created equal had been re-interpreted; to Jefferson and to the idealists among his colleagues this had meant that every man had the right to be as good as his neighbor, but that every man had to achieve equality by his own mental and physical efforts. Many Americans were still loyal to the original beliefs, almost every American held to them in some unthinking corner of his heart, but the right to be as good as your neighbor had become a necessity to be the same as your neighbor. America to the Americans: Heaven on earth! And the angels either have no need to think or else they all think alike. Orthodoxy, the absolute equivalent to Americanism, had become the driving force behind American education. Social and economic life had changed its manner until its principal purpose was to encourage uniformity. Heterodoxy was by nature an un-American activity. The service of ideals that were shared by all Americans became, for the most part, lip service. Democracy, for example: democracy, being the common aim of all Americans and being part of American existence, was a fact. A fact *is*, there is no need to think about it. Thought in itself is unimportant and possibly even dangerous, for thought may lead to heterodoxy. And so in American life bromides took the place of intellectual exercise, scholarship took on an importance that had once belonged to creation: technological advances and the acquisition of money

— the great equalizer — were recognized as man's outstanding achievements.

America had become Europeanized, and the Europe
which she had taken as her model was the Europe of
the nineteenth century, the Europe of decay. But
America had found more efficient means of spreading
rottenness than had ever been known to the Europe
she copied. America had Hollywood making its ninety-
minute bromides to persuade an audience that happiness or misery, liberty or oppression, can be carried
and explained in the length of one film.

The superficial products of Hollywood's ubiquitous
influence are obvious. We can think of England, where
the language takes on American crispness and American inflection, and, by the way, this may save the
English language from premature sterility; or we may
remember a drive through a Continental village and
contrast the color — for instance of the girls' dresses —
the spruceness and the cheerfulness of its life today
with the drabness of even twenty years ago. The difference, I suspect, is testimony to Hollywood's service
as mirror to millions who have never before studied
themselves in a glass.

When Hollywood is held responsible for a hideous
increase in the numbers of juvenile delinquents, should
one not remember the time when Sexton Blake was
in the dock on the same charge, and is it possible that

our grandfathers blamed Porthos, Athos, and Aramis
for the sins of little Victorians? Or that their grandfathers shook their heads when young Nell was hanged
for stealing sixpence, and moaned, with unctuous
pleasure, that it all comes from seeing *The Beggar's
Opera?* As keeper of the people's morals, Hollywood
has been far more careful than the authors of popular
literature. Nowhere but in Hollywood does virtue in-
evitably triumph, only in Hollywood does vice always
lead to destruction. Hollywood may have changed the
custom of delinquents; it is in no way responsible for
the delinquency. The way of life described in American films can make Europeans envious, and this envy
has been the cause of much ill-feeling against the
Americans. But the error of Hollywood is not that it
has encouraged Europe to covet physical comforts that
are in Europe either difficult or impossible to get, but
rather that it has offered no mental standards to sup-
port the physical standards that it advertises so successfully. The changes and charges that I have men-
tioned — and many like them — are superficial, but the
thoughtlessness with which Hollywood has touched
Europe: that is another matter. It is the tragedy of
America and of Europe that Hollywood has set itself
the task of boosting American virtue at just that point
where America's virtue has become America's vice:
in the ease of American life. It is tragic both for
America and for Europe that, by persistent proclama-

tion of the delights of orthodoxy, Hollywood has made more difficult the task of the rebel: the rebel in the mass and the rebel in the individual.

Not, of course, that Hollywood has never concerned itself with philosophical, political, or sociological questions; and it may seem churlish in me that having attacked Hollywood for encouraging thoughtlessness I should then attack Hollywood when it attempts to encourage thought. But the seemingly thoughtful films of Hollywood serve my thesis even more effectively than the froth. Man's devotion to print was dangerous enough; man's devotion to pictures is even more likely to bring disaster to his mental processes. It is always difficult to question the evidence of the eyes: solutions observed through the senses seem far more convincing than solutions contrived by the brain. The cinema, both because it is commercial and because it is — quite rightly — primarily an entertainer, cannot involve itself in all the inflections of debate. It is said that twenty million people must see one film before that film pays its way; the film-maker, if he is to be successful, must equate the intelligence of his film with the lowest intelligence among that twenty million. The lowest intelligence can only be shown black and white, good and evil. Such simple exposition is possible when simple problems are handled, but then few of the problems of the world are simple.

America has offered political, economic, and even

military leadership to Europe. Yet Europe needs more, for Europe's troubles are not at all only physical. Europe needs a democracy equivalent to Jefferson's optimistic faith "that men may be trusted to govern themselves without a master. . . ." This was America's democracy once; now America's democracy has become orthodoxy and complacency. Europe needs America's democracy as it was, not as it is. Europe needs, above all, to rediscover the ability to think. And, in a way that Europe as a whole has never known and America as a whole has long forgotten, Europe needs to exercise that ability in the millions of the newly half-educated. We need the voice of Thomas Jefferson and we have been given the voice of Hollywood. There are still Jeffersons in the United States. In America far more than elsewhere, man is still capable of questioning and diverting man's destiny. Hollywood has trapped some of the rebels; but outside Hollywood, there are rebels still, though they have no medium as powerful as Hollywood by which to reach Europe.

But how can we discover them?

They are not among the authors of popular fiction. The cult of the happy ending, and the equally vicious cult of easy tears, is followed by American readers with such devotion that the American writer must either conform — and become a best-seller — or rebel, fling himself to the opposite extreme, and, losing all moderation in indignation and distaste, there revel in abnormalities. And popular writing, the kind of American writing that is best known in Europe, is becoming more and more the product of a New York suburb of Hollywood, written by men who have one eye turned towards the West Coast and one hand held out hopefully for Hollywood riches.

We might have discovered them, these thinking Americans, among the soldiers who were with us during the war, but there is an essential difference between the soldier and the civilian that he was before he put on uniform. Strange surroundings, excitement, the loneliness and the frustrations of overseas service make soldiers more typical of armies than of any one nation, and, in addition, so many of the G.I.'s supporting Rainbow Corner gleaned their ideas of America from the same source whence so many of us gleaned ours: from Hollywood.

The true voice of America can still be heard in her philosophers and her poets, but it is now no exaggeration to say that only a philosopher can read philosophy and that only poets do read poetry. It can be heard among America's teachers — the depressed class in America's predominantly commercial society — but, partly because American scholarship has won and often deserved a reputation for being anything but inspired, and partly because, particularly in England, we have a ridiculous and snobbish attitude to American educational values, few of us can get within the preaching range of an American educator.

Sometimes, but not often, a Jeffersonian echo rings out from Congress, and sometimes from the White House. We are forced to listen, eager for some vague but heartening indication of the genuine America. Holding suspect the popular media — and mistrusting above all the sham voice of Hollywood — we must strive to seek out for ourselves and convert to our own use the mainsprings of American rebellion: the books, the letters, and the speeches of the Americans who are the real American tradition. If we cannot discover America's rebels, we must be content with resurrecting the inspiration of their rebellion, and then by establishing the worthiness of the American past, we may be able to apply its healthy individualism to our own needs.

Hollywood has been blamed for encouraging Europeans to covet physical comforts that are in Europe impossible of acquisition, but if we are to envy America it is not for the comfort and luxury of American life. As early as 1787, Thomas Jefferson realized that these, the very things in American society that are unenviable, might eventually prove inimical to the success of the American ideal. It was then that he wrote: "The people cannot be all and always well informed. The part which is wrong will be discontented . . . if they remain quiet . . . it is a lethargy, a forerunner of death to the public liberty. . . . God forbid that we should ever be twenty years without such a rebellion . . ."

Europe must rediscover rebellion: the excitement of individual mental adventure and the thrill of revolt against the easy doctrine of complete explanation and against the easy satisfaction of the perfect solution. America, with Hollywood as its teacher and as its voice, has accepted a new doctrine of Divine Grace and has learned to prefer a national to an individual salvation; to this America the mind of one man is necessarily inferior to the mind of the millions and the decision of the millions is complete and predigested before Hollywood interprets it to the individual. We, in Europe, need to revive the habit of asking questions; Hollywood has taught us to be content with answers. If we are to envy America it is for the fact that, despite the oppression of ease, America still has her pioneers and her rebels.

5

REVOLUTION IN MUSICAL TASTE

Martin Cooper

In addition to music criticism for the London *Daily Herald, Daily Telegraph,* and *The Spectator,* MARTIN COOPER has written several books in the field, including a study of French music between 1870 and 1925.

MARTIN COOPER

Revolution in Musical Taste

Music lost its aristocratic character in the first half
of the nineteenth century. A revolution in taste took
place and like all revolutions, aesthetic as well as social,
it aimed at the enfranchisement of a new element, in
this case the bourgeoisie. It was bourgeois taste that
found expression in the spectacular excesses of French
grand opera and in the respectable "family" romanti-
cism of Schumann and Mendelssohn. Beethoven and
Berlioz wrote for a still wider public, an idealized hu-
manity which may not have existed but was in any
case the direct antithesis of Stendhal's "happy few."

Now, in the twentieth century, the revolution has
gone a step further. With the enormously increased
diffusion of music brought about by all kinds of me-
chanical means, the common man has joined the
audience. It is his taste that determines the character
of the greater part of music now written. Not, of course,
of that minute fraction that we call "good" or "serious"
music, which stands at the opposite extreme to the
popular, but of the music published by the big commercial publishing houses.

The democratization of taste has gone far further in America than in Europe and has indeed spread to Europe from America. Serious American composers — Sessions, Piston, Schuman, Copland, Virgil Thomson, and Roy Harris — are pioneers of European musical movements in the New World. Their artistic formation was European and even when they retrieved a really personal or — if there is such a thing — a really American style, they played no reciprocal part in influencing the music of Europe.

On the creative side, then, we can discount American influence, and America's creative poverty partly explains, as it has also qualified, that concentration on performance natural among a people preoccupied with means rather than ends. Bertrand Russell has spoken of the Americans' lack of aesthetic sense, produced by an excessive preoccupation with utility. And in fact America has been remarkable in every way of life for the elaboration of techniques and a comparative indifference towards the ends to which those techniques are applied.

The big American orchestras have set a standard of purely technical performance, not necessarily of interpretation, for the whole world. The grouping of the best players, either European or only American by a generation or two, under the best European conductors has produced a smooth efficiency and an opulence of manner which Americans take for granted in all aspects of life. In fact, the position in America today is the exact reverse of that in Vienna during the first quarter of the last century. There, musical creation was at the highest level that it has reached anywhere at any time, with Haydn, Schubert, and Beethoven all active. But there was no orchestra capable of giving even a satisfactory performance of their works — certainly none that would bear any comparison, from the purely technical point of view, with the great American orchestras of today.

The absence of a strong and independent creative element in American musical life has allowed the emphasis on performance to become quite disproportionate, even among serious musicians; and the quick popularizing and commercializing, copying and eventual distorting, typical of a country where taste is democratized, has had disastrous results. The film industry is the chief agent in this process, of course, but American broadcasting has also played its part. Szigeti, in his autobiography, tells us of how a permanent maximum of golden tone — tone, that is, with the highest possible concentrated "schmalz," or fatty content — is demanded in instrumentalists. Radio engineers will even undertake to correct deficiencies in this matter, often without the knowledge of the artist, so that an unaccompanied Bach suite for violin may appear with a super-gloss finish or a gipsy throb.

The devastating influence of the microphone on

singers is not, of course, a specifically American phe-
nomenon, but it is mainly in Hollywood and as film
actors or actresses that indifferent singers have been
built up into kings and queens of song. More serious
in its effect on the art of singing, easy success and big
money in the film world have tempted young singers
to dispense with the long training and apprenticeship
served by the great singers of the past. A newly discovered singer finds that with hardly more than a few
months' training he will be cast for large roles and
earn huge fees. The artificial sweetening, enriching,
and tailoring of the sound track standardizes vocal and
instrumental tone in just the same way as feminine
beauty is standardized; and the standard is set by the
American public, which seems to prefer make-believe
to facts.

Through the moving picture and the phonograph
this whole complex performance-obsession has been
transported to Europe, where it has influenced serious
music and taken complete possession of the entertainment world. Fifty years ago, France, Austria, and England each had their own quite distinct forms of light
music. Think of a Messager *opéra comique,* a Lehár
operetta, or *The Geisha.* National characteristics found
one of their most attractive and least harmful expres-
sions in music so intimately connected with the social
life of each country: the charming, easygoing senti-
mentality of the Viennese operetta, the wit and unpre-

tentiousness of French *opéra comique*, with its strong *côté grivois*, and the unsophisticated popular vitality of the English musical play. Now the fashion for American Negro music has swept away these distinctions. It has imposed comparative uniformity where there was once variety and made the whole world of entertainment music virtually an American appanage.

The influence of American Negro music on serious non-commercial artists never went deep. Debussy played with what now seems a primitive form of it in the "Golliwog's Cake Walk" of his *Children's Corner*, as far back as 1908, but it was not until the first World War that the fashion really started. Poulenc's *Rapsodie Nègre* dates from 1917, and in his memoirs, Darius Milhaud describes his fascination when he heard Billy Arnold's band just arrived from New York, playing at the Hammersmith Palais de Danse in 1920. Milhaud's own ballet, *La Création du Monde*, in 1923, was probably the most distinguished music composed under the Negro influence. Satie had a ragtime number in "Parade"; Auric wrote a foxtrot "Adieu New York"; Stravinsky wrote his ragtime and piano rag music. Even Ravel wrote a blues in his *Violin Sonata* and a parody of the fashionable jazz in his *L'Enfant et les Sortilèges*, while Křenek, in *Jonny Spielt Auf*, written in 1927, carried the new style into the opera house.

The whole movement, if it can be called that, was short-lived, and perhaps the only solid gain to European music was the reappearance of the element of improvisation in the Negro bands. Music had become, and has still remained, too note-bound, too highly organized, with no scope left for the creative instincts of the individual performer. The last traces of creative improvisation disappeared with the great performer-composers of the nineteenth century — Liszt or Rachmaninov, for whom the cadenza in a concerto was still an opportunity for genuine impromptu creation. But with the standardization of the cadenza the player was bound to his book. American Negro bands, with their brilliant improvising trumpeters, clarinetists or saxophone players, reintroduced this element of creativeness: a kind of highly decorated "gagging" comparable with that inspired invention of slang phrases which has been America's most individual contribution to the language. Both have a strong popular flavor and a coarse, ruthless quality which has been their chief recommendation to the tired palates of European connoisseurs.

The fashion for American Negro rhythms and tone combinations was in fact the symptom of a profound shifting of aesthetic values. The center of the disturbance was France, where the utmost pitch of refinement had been reached by Debussy and Ravel and the reaction set in with corresponding violence. The *fureur nègre* was an attempt to escape from the exquisite, the evocative, the scented, the precious, into a world of simple, tough, unpretentious reality. Jean Cocteau, the prophet of the movement, saw it as "an escape from the domination of the Parisienne; from half-lights, muslins, enervating charms and scents," as he puts it, "into a more masculine world of solidly-built, muscular, clean-cut music."

The ideal was anti-romantic, athletic and non-spiritual and the preoccupation with technique and the emphasis on efficiency gave it many affiliations to American ways of thought, or perhaps to America as seen through French eyes. Even the attitude of the young composers to their work was consciously modeled on that of the modern businessman rather than that of the romantic artist; and an American composer who studied during this period in France, Aaron Copland, has taken this attitude home with him. Copland is described by Adolpho Salazar, the Spanish-American critic, as "above all a musical artificer; a worker, who with certain rhythmic, harmonic, melodic and especially sonorous materials, fashions musical goods." This kind of music serves the client who has come to order in the composer's factory a certain amount of music for the theater, the ballet, the radio, or the chamber ensemble.

In his autobiography, Milhaud tells the history of another utilitarian venture, fundamentally American in inspiration and eventually all too successful in America and Europe. This was Satie's idea of *musique d'ameublement* or "furnishing music" — as we say, "furnishing stuffs."

Says Milhaud:

> In the visual realm there are shapes to which no one pays any attention: the design of a wallpaper; the moulding of a frieze or the frame of a looking glass. Satie thought that there might well be music of the same order — "furnishing music" — not meant to be listened to but varying in character according to where it was played.
>
> The future has proved him right. In American cafés there are now machines with which every client can furnish his solitude, or accompany his companions' conversation. Isn't that furnishing music — the sort one hears without listening to it?

If the habit of laying on music, like hot and cold water, was the fulfillment of Satie's ideal, American influence has brought it back to Europe again, increased a hundredfold and now forming one of the most serious obstacles to the formation of popular taste.

The same utilitarian ideal in a rather different form appeared simultaneously in Germany, in the *Gebrauchsmusik* or "music for use," sponsored for a time by Hindemith, Weill, and the younger composers generally. At the same time the beauty of the machine found something approaching genuine aesthetic expression in Honegger's "Pacific 231" and a naïve naturalistic imitation in Mossolof's "Iron Foundry" or "Music of the Machines." Long before, in 1914, the

Italian Futurist musician, Luigi Rossolo, had written his "Four Networks of Noises." "Why cling," he says, "to Bach and Beethoven when the city is alive with the purring of motors, the pounding of pistons, the screeching of gears, the roar of forges, mills, printing presses and underground railways?" And Rossolo, starting from the Negro practice of tapping, clacking and gurgling, devised six families of noises: booms, whistles, whispers, screams, percussion noises, and sounds made by animals and human beings.

This ideal of the industrialization of music, whether in its French, German, or Italian form, was of transatlantic inspiration and from industrialization to commercialization was a small step.

At every level then, American influence on music in Europe has had the same characteristics. The spectacle of American life suggested to the European composer a new utilitarian or functional ideal of music, while American musical performance has popularized a streamlined, smooth glamor. Both represent the eruption of popular urban taste into musical aesthetics, a taste incapable of appreciating subtleties of thought or feeling but eager for sensation, rhythms that titillate, and that slick, sweet, warm, and juicy tone quality, melody and harmonization, which we associate with the cinema organ and the multitudinous orchestras representing as nearly as possible the cinema organ's characteristics.

This democratization of taste has had its effect on the interpretation of American classical orchestras. They tend, except under the most inflexibly purist European conductors, to show a slickness of phrasing, sensational dynamics, an undifferentiated sweetness of tone and a general air of machine-turned finish which emphasize the surface qualities of the music at the expense of the inner quality of the work.

There is one branch of musical life in which American citizens, at least by adoption if not by birth, have excelled in recent years — in musical scholarship or musicology. Einstein, Bukofzer, Reese, and many other scholars have transplanted the Germanic tradition of learning to America, and they and their pupils have produced valuable, often monumental, studies of various eras, genres, or personalities in musical history. Facts in these American works of scholarship are often effectively presented and forcefully, if somewhat arbitrarily, interpreted. But the element of discussion, a resilient give-and-take between author and reader, is absent.

There is a certain simplicity about many works of American scholarship, a naïve and rather too manifest delight in specialized knowledge and a lack of humane, literary quality in the presentation of facts. This is partly a Germanic legacy, no doubt, and so unfortunately is the literary style, bristling with Germanisms already affecting English musical writing. Thus "voice leading" takes the place of the English "part writing"; "to stem from" replaces "to derive from"; "notes" become "tones" and heavy adjectives, such as "accompanimental," are coined in order to translate unwieldy German composite nouns. These commonplaces of American writing about music are already forming an English musical jargon.

It is not fair to put the whole blame on German scholarship for an exclusive concentration on facts and an unwillingness to discuss their interpretation from the point of view of general culture. Scholarship is, of course, a means — not an end. The annotated catalogue or the dictionary of sources is an instrument of the understanding. To confuse it with the understanding is to confuse the means with the end; and if the lesser American musical scholars — and I am certainly not speaking of the chief figures — have tended to concentrate on this first stage, if their interpretation of fact is sometimes arbitrary or callow, they are, after all, only repeating the pattern which is to be found in every walk of American life — the preference for technique to creation, for the process to the subject, for the means to the end.

And so our view of American influence on European music must really depend, in the last resort, on our attitude to the democratization of taste. Can a whole new uneducated public be aesthetically enfranchised without lowering aesthetic standards? If not, then

American influence has been harmful, for it has already begun the scaling down of aesthetic values so as to be within the intellectual grasp of the average city dweller, beside whom Stendhal's "average sensual man" would have seemed highly civilized.

This is a revolution not merely in taste but in the very concept of taste: the acceptance of the fatal division of society into high-brow and low-brow as a necessary stage in the process which will end, not with the debasement of taste, but with the disappearance of the word from our vocabulary. And yet perhaps the most hopeful signs of a change of direction are in America itself. No country, not even England, possesses a more informed and critical minority, more aware of the shortcomings of their own civilization or more determined to cure them. There is a strong movement of anti-materialist feeling in America today; and if no single critic of the American people comparable in power or stature to Goethe has yet appeared, the combined efforts of a large number of lesser men may still achieve what, after all, Goethe's flaying of the German character never achieved, a fundamental change of direction.

6

THE REIMPORTATION OF IDEAS

Perry Miller

Professor of American literature at Harvard University, PERRY MILLER is the author of several books, including a major study of Jonathan Edwards. During 1949-50 he was a visiting professor at the University of Leyden, The Netherlands.

PERRY MILLER

The Reimportation of Ideas

As the only American participant in this series, I
start under the grave handicap imposed by Bertrand
Russell when he declared the American vocabulary
to be insufficient, and our pronunciation blurred. I am
bound to assume, therefore, that my style and my
syntax are unpleasant to the British.

Of course, I might retort that certain British manners
of speech — not all and never the Scottish or the Welsh,
but a few others — do fall upon American ears with
something less than felicity. On this score mutual re-
crimination could continue endlessly and no impact
whatsoever in either direction would be registered.
Fortunately, Bertrand Russell does concede one, although only one, good thing to the American language
— its slang. Perhaps if I fall back from time to time
on this, my native argot, I may be found just tolerable.

First off I am struck by the way the five foregoing
papers testify to the immensity of the American impact; I am the more fascinated because here and
there the acknowledgment is made, by those whose
disposition towards America may be called friendly,

81

in what to my American sense is a noticeably grudging tone. I certainly do not wish to affect a cleverness I do not possess, but to my apprehension, coming to the discussion with an array of frankly American sensitivities, the papers reveal more than they explicitly say. They seem, in short, to be skirting the subject, and fumbling for critical devices to minimize what inwardly they confess is gigantic.

I hope I may be allowed to say this not out of chauvinism or out of 100 per cent Americanism. No one more than I deplores some aspects of the American effect upon Europe, or of the American behavior in Europe. No one is more eager to rally Europe to stand on its own venerable feet. All I ask is whether these discussions are directed toward what America actually is exporting in the form of cultural influence, and not toward fantasies of wholly European construction. Which perhaps is another way of asking whether there really does exist a Europe that can any longer be rallied against the more terrifying of American influences, or that can profit by the more liberating.

For example, I heartily agree with Mr. Martin Cooper that a revolution in aesthetic taste was enacted in the nineteen century, and that today that revolution is carried further in America than in Europe. However, when he insists that in American broadcasts the sound track is artificially sweetened in just the same way as feminine beauty is standardized, I must turn to the lingo sanctioned by Bertrand Russell and cry "Boloney." When he argues that the machines in American cafés exist only for what Satie calls "furnishing music" — that is, the sort one hears without listening to — let me assure him that he has failed to grasp the vital role of the juke box in American culture. You don't put your nickel in, mister, until you've made up your mind what you want to hear. Mr. Cooper finds all this illustrative of the American preference for make-believe, and of a refusal to face facts.

I am compelled at this point to lament the truly baneful influence of the American movies. It is not what they do to the American mind, which forgets the film five minutes after leaving the theater, but the effect they have upon the liberal-minded European who has not yet appreciated how the Americans take even their fairy stories in a highly Pickwickian sense.

What these papers do reveal, as much in what I hold their misconceptions of America as in their penetrating recognitions, and above all in their generous expectancy of the still to be realized possibilities, is the astonishing fact that America exerts and for a long time will exert upon Europe an influence that must be called revolutionary. This fact would be clear enough were it not that language itself confuses the picture. There is only the one word "revolutionary" to describe both the challenge directed against the order of Western Europe by socialism or Marxian communism, and that implied at every point by the ordinary way of living in America.

Because in Europe "left-wing" now means socialism, Bertrand Russell implies, America becomes on the plane of economic theory or of social ideology the citadel of conservatism. Leaving aside for the moment the problem of the real sources of the American obsession with the peril of communism, of what I regret to state often does approach an hysteria, but which may also be interpreted as the American way of manifesting a determination to extend the revolution that began with the Declaration of Independence — leaving aside, I say, the abstractions supposedly aligned in the cold war, I think it evident from these papers that, on the simple day-to-day level of life as it is lived, America continues to disturb and frighten and prod Europe. It excites simultaneously both revulsion and envy. It is still the land that gives or is ready to give the common man what he wants, be that good or bad. All too often European criticism of America is a transparent effort to deny to the common man in Europe what he, transported to America, believes he has achieved or can achieve.

America is a perpetual declaration that Western European society can become open-ended if it tries. Men can be mobile and careers be open to talents. Violence and vulgarity, improvised jazz, philosophical pragmatism, and decent bathrooms are so many declarations of man's mastery of his resources. And this mastery — here is the American contention — is as possible in Europe as in America. It is as possible because America is Europe working out, still in the process of working out — far as yet from attaining — ambitions that were conceived and cradled in Europe.

For this reason I am enormously cheered by the sane words of Bertrand Russell on the subject of American bathroom civilization.

Let it be said, once and for all, that for Americans good plumbing is like good health. It's a wonderful thing to have but something you talk about only when you don't have it. Repeated visits to Great Britain have long since persuaded me that the man who invented the geyser should be pilloried in every history of the nineteenth century as the arch betrayer of modern civilization. He gave to what in England are called, I believe, the lower-middle classes the fatal illusion that they possessed a modern convenience, with the result that Europe was cheated of the revolution it should have had, the revolution in which the ordinary citizen would have demanded of an industrial order that he share in the benefits of industrialism. Hence communism and all its woes.

By the same token I am not at all cheered, but rather deeply depressed, by Mr. Morpurgo's adoption of the facile distinction between the America of Thomas Jefferson which he says — and I agree — Europe is in need of, and the comfort and luxury of American life for which, he declares, you are not to envy the Americans. I object to this disjunction, not so much for the sake of America as for the sake of the Western tradition which is Europe's and America's. It is a false antinomy. America may indeed pose the problem of whether man is to conquer the gadget or be conquered by it, but America only poses most precisely what is the inescapable problem. In America it is still a fifty-fifty proposition — what Britisher wants better fighting odds? In what do we believe? In abundance or scarcity? Or shall it be recorded that England in the rigors of austerity, out of annoyance with Hollywood, so lost its historical perspective as to forget that Thomas Jefferson himself was a copious inventor of gadgets — including the comfortable and luxurious one of the swivel chair?

Let me at any rate assure Mr. Morpurgo and my British friends that American democracy has not become, as he so categorically asserts, orthodoxy and complacency. To say that is utterly to misunderstand the meaning of Franklin Roosevelt, or the election of 1948, or the recent New York election, or of the turmoil of American politics at this moment. It is to forget, as does Mr. O'Faolain in his talk on the Irish immigrant, the yeoman service done by the Irish machine politician in the New Deal. Or indeed the part that the Irish political bosses have in fact played in teaching American Anglo-Saxons the responsibilities of a democracy toward the poor and bewildered newcomer in a teeming city. Somebody had to look after him. I do not mean that the boss was the ideal solution. The point is that the framework of urban government we inherited from England — the mayor and the city council — proved upon so severe a testing to be inadequate. Someone had to do the job and up to a degree the boss did. The lesson is as important for Europe as for America.

I am trying to say, in other words, that America has mainly been occupied for two or three hundred years with working out the consequences of problems given by Europe. We have had, it is true, one other integer added from non-European sources: the Negro. But Europe of the seventeenth century was already fascinated by the Negro — witness the drawings of Rembrandt. The line from Rembrandt's sketches to the crowded Rotterdam auditorium that last October listened with intensity to Louis Armstrong is direct. Mr. Cooper finds that Negro bands appeal to the tired palates of European connoisseurs. One can report only one's experience and may be deceived by it. Still, in the last few months in Europe I have found an appreciation of Louis Armstrong that does not strike me as limited to tired palates. But indeed the Negro and his music make a special case.

Otherwise it may be suggested that the materials we have had to work with were given us by Europe, chiefly by England but also by all Europe: the people themselves, the Common Law, the King James Bible, Shakespeare, Puritanism, Kantian idealism, Darwin and naturalism, and then two world wars. What we give back, whether it be a movie, or a tank, or pragmatism, or T. S. Eliot, is what we have been able to make out of what was sent us in the first place. For that reason I say that America does press upon Europe, quite apart from what it may now be attempting in the form of a pact or a policy, as a revolutionary force, as a force which Europe cannot deny and cannot evade because America is, as Mr. Lehmann has suggested, the pupil of Europe.

It is in fact more than pupil — it is bone of the European bone, blood of the European blood. Its demands would not excite such disturbed and divided responses as the discourses in this series have exemplified were it not that Europe recognizes, however warily, the voice as its own. Mr. Lehmann remembers that in his youth the works of Hawthorne, Emerson, and Poe were assumed to have their roots deep in English literature and that their sunflower faces were ever turned towards Europe. Of course they were. But at the same time, from the American perspective the line is as straight as straight can be from Poe to Faulkner, from Hawthorne to Lewis, from Emerson to Hemingway. Between the first three and the second lies a revolution, says Mr. Lehmann. Yes, in a sense.

And yet, in another sense, no revolution at all but rather a steady unfolding of implicit meanings.

"Whoso would be a man," said Emerson, "must be a non-conformist." And again he said: "If I am a Devil's child I shall live from the Devil."

Surely it takes no great penetration to move with the evolving conditions of American society from these propositions to the corollary that the sun also rises, that the non-conforming man will assert by saying "Farewell to Arms" that what is devilish is of the Devil. If Hemingway and Faulkner now exert upon the literature of Western Europe, and even upon cheap paper books in soldiers' barracks and seamen's bunks, a pervasive influence, the reason is not that they are novelties from Mars but a comment of this civilization upon itself which Europe, even if obliquely and reluctantly, recognizes as a comment upon Europe.

Mr. Lehmann notes, as have others, that throughout this modern American literature runs an astonishing prevalence of a hatred for, a revulsion against, their own civilization. To this observation, delivered in such a tone, the puzzled American at first responds, "What else are we here for? Look at all there is yet to be done." Then he hears Mr. Lehmann continue that this revulsion produces cynicism and despair; that this spiritual emptiness is the corrupting influence of American literature. Whereupon the American once again must patiently explain that Sinclair Lewis has castigated George Babbitt not out of contempt but out of love and charity. Must we always, before every *Grapes of Wrath*, every *Winesburg, Ohio*, every *An American Tragedy*, serve notice that Ben Jonson did not exactly view Bartholomew Fair with cynicism and despair, nor did Fielding find the sensual escapades of Tom Jones a sign of spiritual emptiness?

Happily, I find no widespread disposition in England to regard *Wuthering Heights* as the report of a Royal Commission on conditions in agricultural Yorkshire — but there does appear to be one that unfailingly interprets the work of William Faulkner as a sociological treatise on the rural South. Once in a while, just for a change, we Americans would enjoy discussing with our European friends Faulkner's status as a creative artist in the twentieth century, particularly as some of us hold him a great artist, with significances universal enough to be even more relevant to Europe than to the State of Mississippi. By the same token, I suspect that European critics like Mr. Lehmann might profit, when they come to gauging the connection between American society and its literature, by somewhat more penetrating meditations not only on the reasons for our long and criminal neglect of Melville, but still more on the fact that at this juncture in world history, Melville has become for thousands of American students the most contemporary of writers.

The real point at issue, which seems to me to lurk obscurely through these discussions, is not one of cynicism or despair but what I have tried to convey by asking, "What else beside to scrutinize our society are we here for?" In this respect I think it may be said that the American product, although manufactured out of European raw materials, may upon being re-shipped to Europe legitimately be submitted to a highly critical impost.

Whether the American judgment upon society be, as with most movies (not, even in Hollywood, with all), that everything is wonderful; or, with pragmatism, that all can be made wonderful; or, with the recent American literature and as Hemingway contends, that whiskey is better than sex because after finishing the bottle you can always throw it at somebody — whatever the answer, the American mind is committed, to the point, if you will, of monomania, to a preoccupation with the issue of man and society. Not, as Bertrand Russell has remarked, man and God, or man and the stars, and possibly not even with man and himself. This obsession, with all its narrowness and its stridency, with its exclusion of all other modes of speculation, with its contempt for everything that Veblen called "idle curiosity," may justifiably be taken for what America has made out of the cultural heritage. It has utilized what it received from Europe — Calvinism of the seventeenth century and the naturalism of the twentieth — almost entirely for the immediate purpose of constructing and analyzing the social order. The least valuable, because the most perfunctory, part of Emerson's thinking was his metaphysics. The Emerson who still speaks to America is the Emerson who restlessly probed the problem of society and solitude. Allowing for fugitive exceptions, the same theme is the insistent concern of our recent literature. European authors like Graham Greene, Kafka, Elizabeth Bowen owe much of their popularity in America to the fact that they give to American readers a chance to take a momentary holiday from worrying exclusively about whether man and his society can get on together.

Well, much of this may be regrettable, but then wherein does the basic problem of the age reside? There are ways of thinking in which a previous determination of man's relation to God is held the first requirement to any ordering of social and international statutes. Perhaps; but America doubts it. America came into being after two thousand years of majestic speculation, often pursued under fantastic hardships, had not quite resolved such transcendental inquiries. Meanwhile it seems patent that men must live, and it seems even more evident that men cannot live, if the word means anything, as in Europe they survived from 1914 to 1918, and from 1939 to 1945, or as in Europe they struggle to endure today. I can comprehend, though from afar, Bertrand Russell's complaint that Europeans being lectured to by optimistic Americans feel like a suffering patient helpless before the doctor with a bouncing bedside manner. Still more can I comprehend his complaint about the difficulties of presenting a new philosophy to the University of Oxford. Still, there must come a time, if we are yet to live in time, when Europe understands that neither the so-called despair of American novelists nor the smugness of American businessmen means wholly what appears on the surface; but that both alike mean that America without Europe is a forlorn being.

The failures of Europe — I mean specifically the two wars that have all but destroyed it — have meant reversals to every force within America which the others in this series have praised, and have strengthened every tendency they abhor. No American asks of Europe that uniformity which supposedly constrains Americans into orthodoxy and complacency, even though in America I have known thousands neither orthodox nor complacent. Too many of us treasure experiences too delicious to be sacrificed to any theorem of a united Europe, such as a breakfast I once had with a Scottish couple, who read in the morning newspaper of a horrible murder in Wales, who descanted at length upon the depravity of the Welsh, and who then cheerfully agreed, "All the same, I'd rather be Welsh than English." Americans are most solicitous that this comedy

endure. We merely point out that meanwhile there
has come into being Great Britain. In America Scots,
Welsh, and English, along with Poles, Italians, Hun-
garians, Germans, and Italians do make an order — at
least of sorts. Shall mankind forever be cheated of
his heritage because man cannot speak to his fellow
across artificially drawn frontiers? Even in America,
can man ever lift his eyes past the gadgets to the stars,
if he must constantly devise gadgets for Europe's con-
flicts?

In one of the most profound fables for our time,
André Gide (who, incidentally, comprehends as well
as any in Europe the significance of the recent American literature) enacts a conversation between Oedipus
and Theseus which I might, with apologies, vulgarize
into a dialogue between Europe and America. "In
tearing out my eyes," says Oedipus, "in this cruel act
I was driven by some secret need of pushing my fortune to the limit, and of accomplishing a heroic destiny." Theseus replies that he cannot really praise this
sort of superhuman wisdom, although he honors the
nobility of Oedipus. As for himself, he will leave
behind him the city of Athens, and it is his happiness
to think that after him, and because of him, men may
be more happy, better and more free. "I am the child
of this earth," says Theseus, "and I believe that man,
whatever he may be, ought to play with what courage
he has."

Some of us believe that in the last generation we in

America have met Apollyon on the slopes of the hill Difficulty, and though we may not have slain him outright we have battered and bruised him and forced him to speak his real name. He is properly called Isolationism. Perhaps those theologies of the past which have insisted that sin is ineradicable are more nearly true, if Bertrand Russell will permit an American to use the word, than pragmatism. And maybe the amount of isolationism among the Western communities must somehow remain constant. Perhaps, then, if the quantity in America has temporarily diminished, the level in Europe must perforce rise. I will confess that after some months in Europe I am terrified at the amount of it I find in several nations of the West and especially in England. I find it fantastic that the other contributors to this series assume as axiomatic that Europe is exhausted, that it is in decay, that it is tired and disillusioned. No doubt it has, like Gide's Oedipus, affirmed the grandeur of man by horribly mutilating itself, and, like him, may thus have won a kind of celestial recognition. But in every theme, conception, melody, or vision which America took from Europe, which she has reworked and now exports, the fundamental proposition is restated — this sort of behavior may be all very heroic, but it is highly unnecessary. The temptations to despair are many, plentiful enough in America, let alone in Europe; but it is not necessary either there or here that we destroy ourselves.

Index

Abraham, 8
America: atomic physicists in, 17;
capitalism in, 4; Catholic Church
in, 32, 44-46; communism in,
17, 84; conservatism in, 84, 93;
critical minority in, 78; democracy of, 54-56, 60, 86; "fact" in,
11; music in, 67-78; musicology
in, 76-77; radicals in, 3-4; religion in, 9-10, 44-46; reputation
of, in Europe, 3-5, 5-6; social
legislation in, 6; and socialism,
6; "tyranny of the herd" in, 17-
18, 56
American: "bathroom civilization,"
16-17, 85-86; big business, 4;
Christianity, 32; concept of life,
8-19, 91; culture, 18, 24, 27, 32;
education, 56-61; effect on aesthetic standards, 18, 77-78; ideas
reimported to Europe, 82-95;
industrialism, 6, 10; intellectuals, 42; literature, 88-91, 94; influence on European, 24-33;
"materialism," 15-17; music: influence on European, 67-78; Negro, 71-73; movies, 13, 26, 28,
31, 51-54, 69, 83, 91; novelists,
13, 60-61, 93; orchestras, 68-69,
76; philosophers, 61; poets, 61;
public, 17-18; radio, 69-70; record in international affairs, 7; re-
sponse to world of ideas, 6-7;
slang, 14, 27, 72, 81; speech,
13-14, 57, 81; teachers, 61
American Revolution, 55
An American Tragedy, 90
Aneas—Anchises complex, 37
Aristocracy, 16
Armstrong, Louis, 87
Arnold, Billy, 71
Astronomy, 8
Auric, Georges, 71

Austerity, 15
Austria, music in, 70

Bankruptcy, 4
Beethoven, Ludwig van, 67, 69
Behemoth, 10
Berlioz, Hector, 67
Berto, 29
Boston, 9, 38; anti-Semitism in, 43;
St. Patrick's Day in, 41
Bowen, Elizabeth, 33, 92
Boxer Rebellion, 7
Britain, 7, 15, 94; speech in, 81;
tariff in, 7
Brontë, Charlotte, 23
Brontë, Emily, 23; *Wuthering
Heights,* 90
Bukofzer, 76
Bunker Hill, 37-38
Byron, 6

Caldwell, Erskine, 28
Calvinism, 91
Cambridge, Duchess of, 5
Canada, 5
Catholic Church, 44; in America,
32, 44-46
China, 7
Christian: art, 9; humility, 9; liter-
ature, 9; religion, 9
Civil War (American), 45
Cleveland, Grover, 5
Cobden, Richard, 4, 5
Cocteau, Jean, 73
Common Law, 88
Communism, 4, 46; in America, 17,
84; Marxian, 83
Communists, 5, 6; in Ireland, 46
Congress, 17, 62
Connolly, Cyril, 27; *Enemies of
Promise,* 26-27
Conservatives, 5
Cooper, Martin, 66, 82-83, 87

97